Discover the Lead

TRUMPET

Smash Hits

Series Editor: Chris Harvey

Editorial, production and recording: Artemis Music Limited • Design and production: Space DPS Limited • Published 2002

International MUSIC Publications

Introduction

Welcome to DISCOVER THE LEAD, part of an instrumental series that provides beginners of all ages with fun, alternative material to increase their repertoire, but overall, enjoyment of their instrument!

For those of you just starting out, the idea of solo playing may sound rather daunting. DISCOVER THE LEAD will help you develop reading and playing skills, while increasing your confidence as a soloist.

You will find that the eight well-known songs have been carefully selected and arranged at an easy level - although interesting and musically satisfying. You will also notice that the arrangements can be used along with all the instruments in the series – flute, clarinet, alto saxophone, tenor saxophone, trumpet, violin and piano – making group playing possible!

The professionally recorded backing CD allows you to hear each song in two different ways:

- a complete demonstration performance with solo + backing
- backing only, so you can play along and DISCOVER THE LEAD!

Wherever possible we have simplified the more tricky rhythms and melodies, but if you are in any doubt listen to the complete performance tracks and follow the style of the players. Also, we have kept marks of expression to a minimum, but feel free to experiment with these – but above all, have fun!

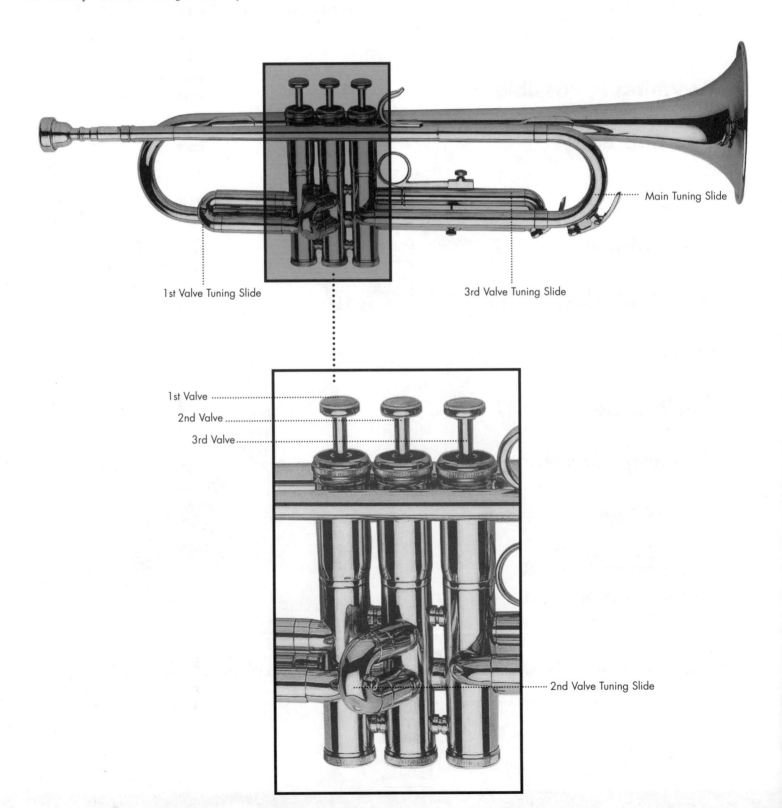

Main Tuning Slide

1st Valve Tuning Slide

3rd Valve Tuning Slide

1st Valve
2nd Valve
3rd Valve

2nd Valve Tuning Slide

Trumpet Fingering Chart

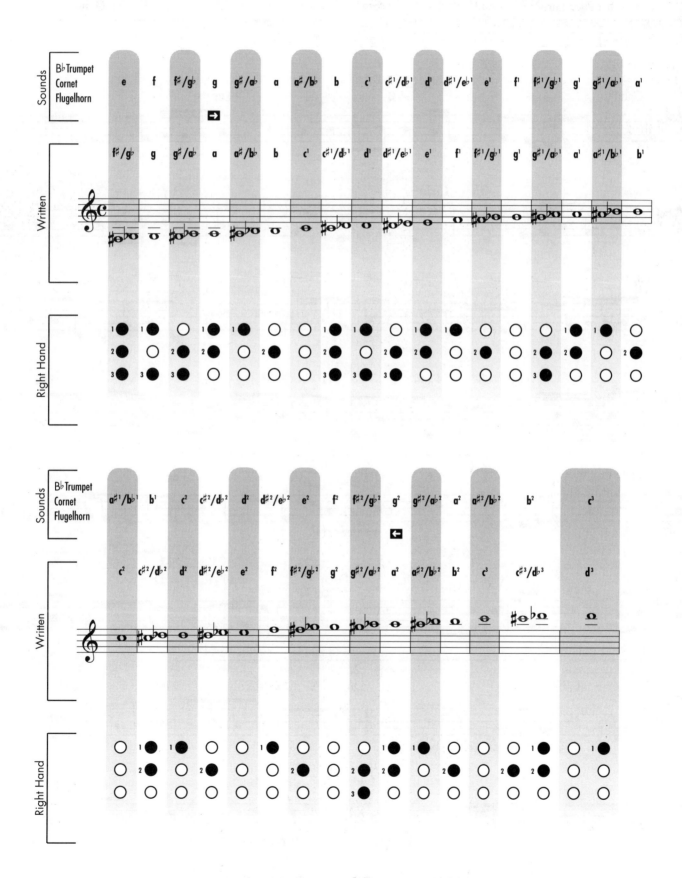

→ Indicates the lower limit of the best playing range

← Indicates the upper limit of the best playing range

Anything Is Possible

Demonstration Backing

Words and Music by
Cathy Dennis and Chris Braide

Demonstration

Backing

Hero

Words and Music by Enrique Iglesias,
Paul Barry and Mark Taylor

Moderately

Bop Bop Baby

Demonstration Backing

Words and Music by
Chris O'Brien, Graham Murphy,
Brian McFadden and Shane Filan

Moderately **Brightly**

Hey Baby

Words and Music by
Bruce Channel and Margaret Cobb

How You Remind Me

Words and Music by
Chad Kroeger, Michael Kroeger,
Ryan Peake and Ryan Vikedal

It's OK

Demonstration

Backing

Words and Music by Mikkel Eriksen,
Hallgeir Rustan and Tor Erik Hermansen

Moderately (swung semi-quavers)

Just A Little

Demonstration

Backing

Words and Music by Michelle Escoffery,
John Hammond-Hagan and George Hammond-Hagan

One Step Closer

Demonstration

Backing

Words and Music by Cathy Dennis,
Mike Percy and Timothy Lever

Brightly

Care Of Your Trumpet

Things You Should Have

Valve oil
Vaseline or slide grease
A brush for the mouthpiece
Flexible swab for the inside
Two cloths for the inside and the valves

Putting Your Trumpet Together

The mouthpiece must be inserted very carefully, as the inside is very delicate and may be damaged easily.

Keeping Your Trumpet Clean

The most effective way to keep your Trumpet working well is to make sure that you keep it clean, inside and out.
You should brush your teeth or rinse your mouth out before playing, as a build up of dirt can affect the Trumpet's performance.

Use a damp cloth to keep the lacquered finish free of fingerprints, but remember never to use normal polish because it will ruin the lacquer. Wash the mouthpiece in warm soapy water about once a week and clean it out with a special brush.

When washing the main part of the Trumpet remember to use warm soapy water and move the valves one by one as the water passes through them. Then rinse your Trumpet through with clean water.

Always lubricate your tuning slides with Vaseline. If the valves start to stick, just unscrew them and add some valve oil.

The springs on the water keys can develop rust, so to prevent this you can occasionally add a small drop of oil.

Storing Your Trumpet

As you are putting your Trumpet in its case always make sure that you have drained the water out and that the mouthpiece has been removed and placed in a separate pouch. Some Trumpet players also loosen the valves to prevent them getting stiff.

A Guide to Notation

Note and Rest Values

This chart shows the most commonly used note values and rests.

Name of note (UK)	Semibreve	Minim	Crotchet	Quaver	Semiquaver
Name of note (USA)	Whole note	Half note	Quarter note	Eighth note	Sixteenth note
Note symbol	𝅝	𝅗𝅥	♩	♪	𝅘𝅥𝅯
Rest symbol	▬	▬	𝄽	𝄾	𝄿
Value per beats	4	2	1	1/2	1/4

Repeat Bars

When you come to a double dotted bar, you should repeat the music between the beginning of the piece and the repeat mark.

When you come to a repeat bar you should play again the music that is between the two dotted bars.

First, second and third endings

The first time through you should play the first ending until you see the repeat bar. Play the music again and skip the first time ending to play the second time ending, and so on.

D.C. (Da Capo)

When you come to this sign you should return to the beginning of the piece.

D.C. al Fine

When this sign appears, go back to the beginning and play through to the Fine ending marked. When playing a D.C. al Fine, you should ignore all repeat bars and first time endings.

D.S. (Dal Segno)

Go back to the 𝄋 sign.

D.S. al Fine

Go to the sign 𝄋 and play the ending labelled (Fine).

D.S. al Coda

Repeat the music from the 𝄋 sign until the ⊕ or To Coda signs, and then go to the coda sign. Again, when playing through a D. 𝄋 al Coda, ignore all repeats and don't play the first time ending.

Accidentals

Flat ♭ - When a note has a flat sign before it, it should be played a semi tone lower.

Sharp ♯ - When a note has a sharp sign before it, it should be played a semi tone higher.

Natural ♮ - When a note has a natural sign before it, it usually indicates that a previous flat or sharp has been cancelled and that it should be played at its actual pitch.

Bar Numbers

Bar numbers are used as a method of identification, usually as a point of reference in rehearsal. A bar may have more than one number if it is repeated within a piece.

Pause Sign

A pause is most commonly used to indicate that a note/chord should be extended in length at the player's discretion. It may also indicate a period of silence or the end of a piece.

Dynamic Markings

Dynamic markings show the volume at which certain notes or passages of music should be played. For example

pp	= very quiet	*mf*	= moderately loud
p	= quiet	*f*	= loud
mp	= moderately quiet	*ff*	= very loud

Time Signatures

Time signatures indicate the value of the notes and the number of beats in each bar. The top number shows the number of beats in the bar and the bottom number shows the value of the note.

YOU'RE THE VOICE

8861A PV/CD

Casta Diva from Norma - Vissi D'arte from Tosca - Un Bel Di Vedremo from Madam Butterfly - Addio, Del Passato from La Traviata - J'ai Perdu Mon Eurydice from Orphee Et Eurydice - Les Tringles Des Sistres Tintaient from Carmen - Porgi Amor from Le Nozze Di Figaro - Ave Maria from Otello

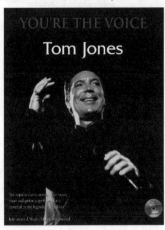

8860A PVG/CD

Delilah - Green Green Grass Of Home - Help Yourself - I'll Never Fall In Love Again - It's Not Unusual - Mama Told Me Not To Come - Sexbomb Thunderball - What's New Pussycat - You Can Leave Your Hat On

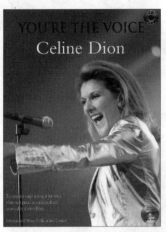

9297A PVG/CD

Beauty And The Beast - Because You Loved Me - Falling Into You - The First Time Ever I Saw Your Face - It's All Coming Back To Me Now - Misled - My Heart Will Go On - The Power Of Love - Think Twice - When I Fall In Love

9349A PVG/CD

Chain Of Fools - A Deeper Love Do Right Woman, Do Right Man - I Knew You Were Waiting (For Me) - I Never Loved A Man (The Way I Loved You) I Say A Little Prayer - Respect - Think Who's Zooming Who - (You Make Me Feel Like) A Natural Woman

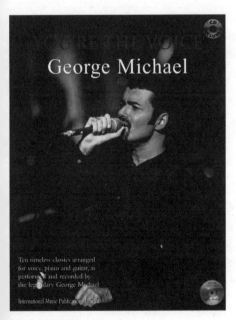

9007A PVG/CD

Careless Whisper - A Different Corner Faith - Father Figure - Freedom '90 I'm Your Man - I Knew You Were Waiting (For Me) - Jesus To A Child Older - Outside

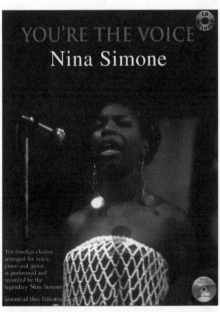

9606A PVG/CD

Don't Let Me Be Misunderstood - Feeling Good - I Loves You Porgy - I Put A Spell On You - Love Me Or Leave Me - Mood Indigo - My Baby Just Cares For Me Ne Me Quitte Pas (If You Go Away) - Nobody Knows You When You're Down And Out - Take Me To The Water

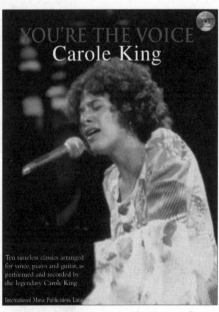

9700A PVG/CD

Beautiful - Crying In The Rain - I Feel The Earth Move - It's Too Late - (You Make Me Feel Like) A Natural Woman So Far Away - Way Over Yonder – Where You Lead - Will You Love Me Tomorrow You've Got A Friend

The outstanding vocal series from IMP

CD contains full backings for each song, professionally arranged to recreate the sounds of the original recording

Karaoke Classics
9696A   PVG/CD   ISBN: 1-84328-202-X

Back For Good - Delilah - Hey Baby - I Will
Always Love You - I Will Survive - Let Me
Entertain You - Reach - New York, New York -
Summer Nights - Wild Thing

Party Hits
9499A   PVG/CD   ISBN: 1-84328-097-8

Come On Eileen - Dancing Queen - Groove Is In
The Heart - Hi Ho Silver Lining - Holiday - House
Of Fun - The Loco-Motion - Love Shack - Staying
Alive - Walking On Sunshine

Disco
9493A   PVG/CD   ISBN: 1-84328-091-4

I Feel Love - I Will Survive - I'm So Excited - Lady
Marmalade - Le Freak - Never Can Say Goodbye
- On The Radio - Relight My - Fire - YMCA - You
Sexy Thing

School Disco
9709A   PVG/CD   ISBN: 1-84328-212-7

Baggy Trousers – Club Tropicana – December
1963 (Oh What A Night) – The Final Countdown –
Karma Chameleon – The One And Only – Material
Girl – Relax – Stand And Deliver – Take On Me